Flip the Flaps

Animal Homes

Judy Allen and Simon Mendez

KINGFISHER
NEW YORK

KINGFISHER
LONDON & NEW YORK

Copyright © 2009 by Kingfisher
Published in the United States by Kingfisher,
175 Fifth Ave., New York, NY 10010
Kingfisher is an imprint of Macmillan Children's Books, London.
All rights reserved.

Distributed in the U.S. and Canada by Macmillan,
175 Fifth Ave., New York, NY 10010

Consultant: David Burnie

First published in hardback by Kingfisher in 2009
First published in paperback by Kingfisher in 2012

Library of Congress Cataloging-in-Publication Data
Allen, Judy.
Flip the flaps animal homes / written by Judy Allen; illustrated by Simon Mendez
p. cm.
Includes bibliographical references and index.
1. Animals—Habitations—Juvenile literature. I. Mendez, Simon, ill.
II. Title. III. Title: Animal homes.
QL756.A45 2009
591.56'4—dc22
2009046930

ISBN: 978-0-7534-6950-7

Kingfisher books are available for special promotions and premiums. For details contact:
Special Markets Department, Macmillan, 175 Fifth Avenue, New York, NY 10010.

For more information, please visit www.kingfisherbooks.com

Printed in China
3 5 7 9 8 6 4 2
2TR/1212/UTD/LFA/128GEMA

Contents

Trees

A tree is a little bit like an apartment building, with homes on every level. Birds and squirrels nest in the branches. Small animals live in cracks in the bark. Woodpeckers may live in a hole in the trunk.

squirrel

4   thrush nest

woodpecker

1. What is a squirrel's nest like?

2. Why do woodpeckers peck wood?

3. Which small animals live in trees?

peppered moth

bark beetle

spider

5

Stones

Big stones are home to small animals that like to live where it is dark and damp. Lift one and you might find earwigs and pill bugs, springtails and centipedes.

thrush

snail

woodpecker
pecking

1. Squirrels build nests, called drays, out of twigs and leaves. Or they may find an empty bird's nest and add a roof.

2. Woodpeckers use their sharp beaks to dig out tasty insects and to make holes for nests.

3. Insects and spiders live on tree bark, and moths rest there, safely hidden.

What lives on tree bark?

peppered moth

bark beetle

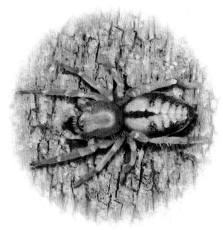

spider

5

Stones

Big stones are home to small animals that like to live where it is dark and damp. Lift one and you might find earwigs and pill bugs, springtails and centipedes.

thrush

snail

1. Yes. The animals come out to eat. Most eat leaves and soggy wood.

2. The spider hides with one foot on the web. A trapped insect will move the web, and the spider will pounce.

3. Worms live in the soil. But if a stone is on top of soil, there might be worms underneath.

earwig

centipede

ladybug flying

Other animals under stones

worm

millipede

springtail

Burrows

A fox's home is called a den. It is a burrow where the female fox has her cubs. She does not make a nest, so the cubs all sleep on the bare ground. Adult foxes mostly sleep outside.

fox cubs playing

1. Do all foxes live in burrows?

2. Are foxes good at digging burrows?

3. Do other animals live in burrows?

Inside a prairie-dog burrow

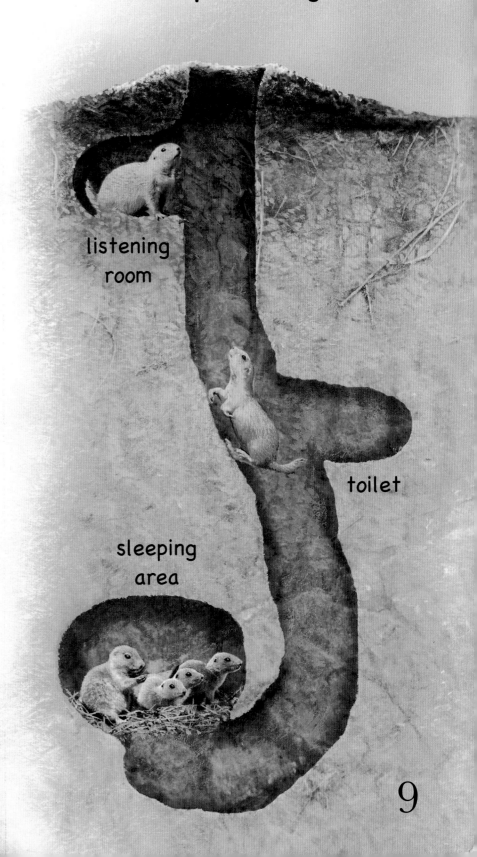

listening room

toilet

sleeping area

Ponds

Ponds are like tiny worlds.
Dragonflies hover above
while their young live below.
Water boatmen and pond
skaters live on the surface.
Beetles dive. Tadpoles
hatch and turn into frogs.

dragonfly

frog spawn
(eggs)

diving
beetle

water snail

tadpoles

1. No. Tadpoles hatch from eggs, become froglets, and climb out. Adult frogs live on land and in ponds.

2. Dragonflies lay their eggs on pond plants underwater. The nymphs hatch and live in the pond for two years.

3. Some can. Others, like the diving beetle, take an air bubble down with them.

dragonfly nymph

A dragonfly nymph changes

A dragonfly!

crawling out of old skin

nymph crawling out of pond

11

Shells

Animals with shells already have homes. Some can go inside their shells and sleep safely. Only the hermit crab doesn't grow its own shell. It finds an empty one to move in to.

hermit crab

Lobsters and mussels also have shells.

1. When
a shell
shrivels
empty

2. A herm
shells o
the crab
find a l

3. No. As
shells are
bodies a
with the

hermit crab n
in to a new

1. Why are the
shells empty?

2. Where do hermit crabs
find the empty shells?

3. Do turtles change
their shells when they
need bigger ones?

s shell grows with it

have
hells.

ell grows
er and
der.

Caves

There are sea caves, ice caves, and land caves where bats may live. Some bats sleep in cracks, and others sleep upside down.

bat

14

1. When an animal with a shell dies, its body shrivels up and an empty shell is left.

2. A hermit crab finds empty shells on the sea floor. As the crab grows, it has to find a larger shell.

3. No. As with snails, their shells are part of their bodies and grow bigger with them.

hermit crab moving in to a new shell

A snail's shell grows with it

Young snails have small, soft shells.

The shell grows bigger and harder.

Caves

There are sea caves, ice caves, and land caves where bats may live. Some bats sleep in cracks, and others sleep upside down.

bat

1. When do bats sleep?

2. Is it cold in a cave?

3. What else lives
   in a bat cave?

Other animals in a bat cave

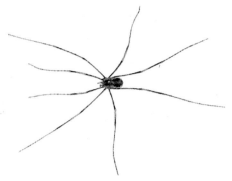

daddy longlegs

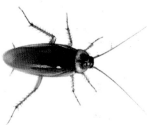

cockroach

cave cricket

cave beetle

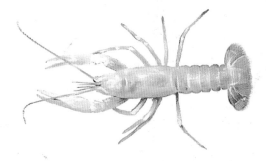

cave crayfish

15

Homebuilders

Beavers use branches and stones to build a lodge in a river or lake. They can bite right through trees with their sharp teeth and chew the wood into useful lengths.

beaver lodge

16

1. Where is the entrance to the beaver lodge?

2. Do beavers eat fish?

3. Do other animals build homes?

1. The lodge entrance is underwater.

2. No. Beavers eat plants, twigs, and tree bark. They store food in the water around the lodge or in a room inside it.

3. Yes. Birds, squirrels, and bees all build homes. The tailorbird makes a home by sewing leaves together.

A tailorbird builds a nest

sewing together leaf edges

safe in the nest

17

Index